From a Spit Seed

From a Spit Seed

Poems by

Wendell Hawken

© 2025 Wendell Hawken. All rights reserved.
This material may not be reproduced in any form, published,
reprinted, recorded, performed, broadcast,
rewritten or redistributed without
the explicit permission of Wendell Hawken.
All such actions are strictly prohibited by law.

Cover design by Shay Culligan
Cover image by Matthew Klein
Author photo by Matthew Klein

ISBN: 978-1-63980-829-8

Kelsay Books
502 South 1040 East, A-119
American Fork, Utah 84003
Kelsaybooks.com

Acknowledgments

Gratitude to these publications that supported my work:

Alchemy and Miracles Anthology (Gilbert and Hall Press, 2023): "Fourteen Couplets in Search of a Water-Torture, Love Your Neighbor Title"
Clarke's Great Outdoors: "Hawk"
KAIROS Literary Magazine: "Two B-52s Overhead"
Making Waves: West Michigan Review: "On the Kitchen Loveseat, Reading Wislawa Szymborska" as "On the Loveseat"
The Midwest Quarterly: "Wheat Straw for Bedding Horse Stalls"
Pink Panther Magazine: "Morning in Montego Bay"
Rockvale Review: "Kitchen Window"
Sequel (Finishing Line Press, 2019): "The Ruby Throats Remember their Flowers, How Long Each Takes to Refill"
Spring and All Anthology (Sidekick Press, 2023): "Fruitful"
Unleash Lit III: "One Row Ahead: *Fletcher, If You Don't Stop That with Your Sister, You Won't Go to Disney World*"
The Virginia Writers Project: "Watering Pots in Drought"
Troublemaker Firestarter: "Front Porch"
Willowaw Journal: "Fallen Fruit"
Written Tales, Nostalgia: "Waking with Thoughts of My Mother"

"After Anguish" won the Letter Review Poetry Prize.

Gratitude to the greater Warren Wilson MFA alumni community for the friendship and support at our summer "Wally Camps," and especially to Gail Peck, Marie Pavlicek-Wehrli, and Debra Conner who helped me craft many of the poems in this collection.

Contents

Breathe   13

ONE

Wheat Straw for Bedding Horse Stalls   17
Front Porch   20
On the Kitchen Loveseat Reading Wislawa Szymborska   22
Fruitful   24
White House State Dinner   27
If She Had Been a Dog   28
Poetry Daily   29
After Receiving the Email   30
Air This Morning Colder Than Its Number   32
Providence Hospital Nursing School Graduation
    Photo, 1931   33
Hawk   34
Visiting the Zoo   36
Waking with Thoughts of My Mother   37

TWO

Spilt Milk   41
Before the Newborn Knew Its Wild   42
Kitchen Window   43
"Ignorance Is Vastly Underrated."   45
Deep into Present-Day Invisible   47
The Peacock's Tail   48
Journaling Summer   49
Over the New River   52

The Ruby-Throats Remember Their Flowers, How Long Each Takes to Refill	53
As Desire Looks to the Future, Regret Implies a Past	54
Thirteen Couplets in Search of a Water Torture, Love-Your-Neighbor Title	57
Watering Pots in Drought	59

THREE

Girls' School Reunion: The 50th	63
Two B-52s Overhead	64
Motivation and Learning: Psych 205	66
Dormmate Reunion at Betsy's	68
Head-Hunter	69
Out the Kitchen Window, I Find My Dark Side	71
Fallen Fruit	72
One Row Ahead: *Fletcher, If You Don't Stop That with Your Sister, You Won't Go to Disney World*	74
Morning in Montego Bay	75
A Famous Poet Reads at a D.C. Bookstore	77
Atrophied, said the Gynecologist	78
All Day on the Farm	80
After Anguish	83

Notes

Breathe

What exhale does to glass.

The soft cough that came to stay.

Little thoughts of quiet days—
returning robins, for instance,

tapping code, heads cocked to hear
earth's answer.

Every river's pointing finger.

The flat, webbed feet of platitude.

Belief's seeds winnowed into fact
and myth tied to memory's mast

sailing past the lies that bind.

ONE

Wheat Straw for Bedding Horse Stalls

The best comes from the Taylor place
near Lincoln, the field at Thunder Run.

Each bale unfolds openminded
when I slice the twine, shake each flake.

Particles like embers fly from my hands.
I shake fire at the beams of light,

make the *whoosh* of borrowed taffeta,
white slip taffeta I wore pubescent proud.

Imagine, shaking wheat straw
and my mother's walking

sounding the same, and how I sing
"Rainy Day in Rio" as she did in rain,

as old snow knows its shadows.
Sky lightens into willowware.

The mockingbird's sudden white-flare flight—
grief's like that.

Yesterday, outside the drugstore
a white-haired woman leaning on

who had to be her daughter,
both peering in a prescription bag.

My mother's ERA stickpin,
her World War II Red Cross Nurse's badge,

now mine. In dreams, my steering wheel
might wobble. I might miss the turn. Get lost.

But no more babushkas at the ribbon factory
who bar the door to where I need to be

to take the test.
Here, the old dogs learn,

and 'moon' means full
whether blood or wolf or snow or hunger,

where tomato-eating squirrels dodge
all the old men's pellet guns

and health is not the measure
of how ill the others are,

where a steady, head-first answer
comes to every praying mantis prayer

wandering unmown fields
in human-less surround with two dogs

plus a last-legs cat lifted to her food,
hands idling on seedheads,

nudging kernels from pods
to fall into their futures.

Do flies know they once were maggots
because their tastes remain the same?

Front Porch

Summer birds that come to breed
now gone to where they go,
their songs a present absence
the tree frogs' August hiss
amplifies.
                Surprising
Michele would call
after my half-glass lapse
after two-hundred-twelve days.

Going out, she calls it.

Didn't taste that great
though I heard myself
think to pour another to discover
if taste got better.
                The cat sits
ears pricked at the shaking
watermelon leaves sprung up
from a spit seed

      **

The something in the cat's mouth
not another newborn rabbit
but a starling
she drops and sits beside
to stare out across the yard.

The bird rights itself, seems
likewise engaged in its horizon
though its starling heart must be
thwack, thwack, thwacking.

The cat perhaps is purring.

From where I sit the picture
of foot-weary tourists
at a bistro table in a village square.

Of long-time lovers anywhere.

On the Kitchen Loveseat Reading Wislawa Szymborska

Waiting for the soda bread to bake its smile,
stroking Gus's coat. There, nestled under Gus's leg,
a tick.
       Wislawa's in Paris. Gus and I are settled in.

Tick legs—unmoving when first plucked
from its cozy suck—begin to wave

and, clever tick, legs up, wriggles its half-bloated
self across the tabletop, upside down.

Wislawa, you would marvel at its flail and squirm.
Find meaning on its hieroglyphic back.
Its steady progress to the edge.

There does seem some Humpty Dumpty
in its fat round self and tiny churning legs.

An easy political to its gray-green bloat.

A tick's a tick. This is a tick, a Lonestar
engorged in Gus's blood.

We will wait here, you in Paris, Gus, the tick, and I
in this rural kitchen until the oven timer bleats
of well-baked soda bread,

and I get up to flush the thing,
or give it grace and chuck it out the door.

Fruitful

In the long sweet not-too-far-back
language from, say, Dr. Williams' chilled plums,
the double dare of eaten peach,

midcentury maraschino cherries bobbing
lonesome in a Midwest fridge,

now the twenty-first century tree-ripe plums
beside a Philadelphia street.
                        No. Not plums.
I checked myself (which more and more
these days I do.)
              It's figs. Figs dirtying the sidewalk
intersection of a named and numbered street.
      You could go there some September
as a pilgrim, a poetic pilgrim
seeking the sweet, soft, red-streaked flesh

because I believe the poem.
If not in life, then license.
                    If you google *fig tree poem*
and can get past Sylvia *sitting*
in the crotch of this fig tree (though prose)
if you resist clicking down Sylvia's path—
too sad for early morning—

                              if you stick with figs,
not the *Ficus religiosa* under which Buddha
found enlightenment, it is *Ficus carica*
you want sticky fingers to stick to,

not necessarily believing
its sap removes warts, softens calluses.

Or its seeds the seeds of understanding,
unity, and truth. Female fertility.

          As a fig leaf is said to cover shame
and in fact now covers Uffizi statuary
penises (thanks to Popes who had the phalluses
chiseled off.)
                    Much to answer for, those popes.

And there's also the knowing
bite in Adam's throat, bob and swallow,
going nowhere.
                    Whereas my mind
more and more the goat going where it will

and turns from news of floods,
bridge collapse, impending war,

                          to fig tree joy
as jumpstart for my own—like begetting like
savoring every fig tree word,
inserting myself beneath that tree
slurping figs with strangers
while in this warm home, both dogs at my feet,
waiting for their walk into a blue snow morning.

        Yesterday, a red fox crossed the yard
slipping here and there on ice
to disappear in the scrub woods flanking the house.

                  How exposed it seemed,
how protective I felt
discovering Sylvia's school-girl
diary and her college letters
there on display in the Grolier Club's glass windows
for anyone who wandered down 60th Street
any time of day or night to read.
Though I read them.
Read every word.

White House State Dinner

Table rounds for ten, golden chargers, apple juice
as wine, photo-ed for continuity, not to touch.

We extras are to chat (harder than it sounds)
and when the presidents start down the stairs
we are to stand,
           applaud,
                      surge forward just a bit.

All day those presidents come down.
That scrap of Chopin from the string quartet.

Ten thousand times Rene Russo, gorgeous in red velvet,
saunters past our table, Clint Eastwood right behind:
Good evening, Agent Raines. You look lovely.
Good enough to eat.

Nine hours times the salaries. Add equipment,
props, food. The twenty grand to rent this place.
All those drafts.
                Revisions.
                        Re-worked words.

If She Had Been a Dog

after Steven Dobyns' "Toward Some Bright Moment"

The woman shuffled behind the man's loud hissing,
You can walk faster than that! Just come on.
Will you come on now? You're not trying.

He had a cane, boxed leftovers, a tidy white goatee,
seeming oblivious to the small crowd
gathering in the restaurant lot

as she slid one foot, the other,
inching along, watching her own walking.
No purse. Amish-like skirt. Sturdy shoes.

If she had been a dog, my friend said later,
we would have intervened.
                              I wonder,
and flash to the Dobyns poem of witnessing
an old blind man kick his dog. Poetry will do that.
The poem's finding took some doing

and though the blind part right, the one
who kicks and curses the cringing Shepherd mutt
not old. And not a man.
                       Well, hello there,
you old biased darlings, you.
What a surprise, meeting here. Like this.

Poetry Daily

I will keep
today's poem open,
the piece with dirty fingernails
and metaphor pulled from a poet's pocket
to tie up all her losses,

will re-read
today's still open poem
if I get the turkey brined, dogs walked—
my daughter's two plus mine—
mashed potatoes done,

ignoring
the mental arrow
down the potato's path to Irish famine,
Carbon County coal mine ancestors
on my mother's side

but will stick
with today's open poem,
maybe leave its link up overnight
to see if—like fireflies in childhood's jars—
it's still alive come morning.

After Receiving the Email

      A Paris garret. A guy known from home. I left for Nice
the next day   and that was that. Still, was glad to know
before opening   his headshot in Obits.

      And for some reason   began to think about
another man   all that Sunday   doing yardwork, weeding,
mulching flower beds.

      Have heard these recognitions   often mutual.
For me at least   him walking down the hall,
shoulder-length dark   blonde dirty (usually a turn-off) hair,

jeans and collared shirt   eye contact brought
a groin throb   as I stood waiting for   the workshop
(throb right now writing this.)

      Turned out, he was its teacher. Kind. Generous.
Edgy in a sweet way. We never had   a one-on-one, then
or at later conferences.

      And now, him long dead,   I wish I had said *Yes*—
having agreed   those younger times—*(see above)*
to share the joint he offered.

      If I had, maybe   I could tell you   if he made
love the way he read: all in   exuberant   joyful
(cocksure comes to mind)   voice high and wide,   hair

swaying,   hands gripping the podium   leaning into
words going   where I never quite   imagined   but, on arrival,
recognize   eyes watering   at the bright light

speed with which I read   the Facebook post:
his name with *Memorial* . . .
and maybe,   it was just a joint he offered.

Air This Morning Colder Than Its Number

When the mind is thinking, it is talking to itself.
                              —Plato

Walking on my fun-house stilt-legged shadow,
hands in pockets, arms like handles, scarecrow hat,

early light slanting orange across bare trees,
both dogs outlined white, the belly of the redtail,

a slight pink stain on snow where the hawk took off,
grasped prey trailing.
              Goodbye, little rodent.
Some have said, and say, you exist for this.

Then a rainbow rose up straight as a flaming sword,
its arc a slow-motion reveal while a second

more muted rainbow appeared parallel above
and because of last year's color class I knew the gray

between the two not darker, the below not lighter,
but another mere illusion on a flat gray morning sky.

Providence Hospital Nursing School
Graduation Photo, 1931

Twenty young women in two lines, short to tall,
flanking a Sister of Charity's bat-winged wimple,

their nurses' pins left-breasted, precisely so,
on starched white uniforms,
                                    and the blondest is my mother,
the left line's second-tallest, squinting at the sun

who grew up poor, eating squirrel and deer
her father shot in Carbon County, Pennsylvania,

who took nurse's training to get her B.S.,
                                    slowly now,
my mother second from the end, slim-waisted, sturdy shoes,

her finger slides face to face, my mother names the names,
who married whom, alive or not, almost talking to herself

what she knew of these women, smiling, pinned, ready
for the wounded.

Hawk

Lowbrow clouds of cotton candy
unspun across the sky—

the day's pink start
amplifies the hum of Interstate 81,

the vague rumble of freight steel on steel,
cross-track bleat of air horns.

If you could walk the lane with me,
the dogs and me, you would see yourself

how the fescue's green turns caramel.
The white glaze night frost lays on pasture,

a sight Vaughn called *new snow.*
Can almost hear him say it: *new snow.*

It's not that I disdain your concrete,
your rise of soldered steel, the jostling.

I know its jolt and drive, neon's night
excitements, the high heel beat on pavement—

did I really walk that way?—

but here, twice now, a female red-tail
sat perched on the fence, not ten feet away

unmoving as I drove down the lane—
eye to her fierce unflinching eye.

Visiting the Zoo

This poem will not bite in spite of any vague
Resemblance it may have to teeth
In its uneven
Ramble across a flat white world.

If this reassurance fails,
Do the math:
Miss Fenstermacher and her kind
(*her ilk,* my mother's voice)
Gone by now: their collared housecoats—
Remember housecoats?—hairnets,
Wooden rulers striking upturned palms.

Believe me, this poem is more afraid of you.
See how it sends its words out into the vast unsullied white
Before its timid scuttle
Back to upper
Case from which it came,
Casting and re-casting for a living bite
While clinging to the shore.

Waking with Thoughts of My Mother

You might have liked it here
what with your capacity for solitude,

liked how night holds on in a thinning linger
you might recognize.

Or the background hum some few miles off
of the north/south interstate.

                          Always the early riser,
you would have enjoyed shadows' hold on
old snow in shapes of house, barn, hay barracks,

and might have stood beside me as heifers'
purple tongues curled around their morning
sweet feed.
                They say the Irish love of land
comes from deprivation.
                        Rooted to your urban corner lot,
you tended your pink-tinged Peace Rose,
and your favorite deep red Mister Lincolns.

You might have liked the way
the starling flock brings a winter tree to leaf,

then levitates the tree-shape
before flying off. The way you left.

TWO

Spilt Milk

Sip the milky drink / a mother's laugh
burbles with the pour / dip and drink

(childhood's duck) / the spill of milk
and the mother / dancing out the door.

A warm white after-sky / the mother
out there / somewhere.

The good-bye / of her lullabies
hangs on the brambles / blackberry

blossoms white / as cloud-words
rambling left to right / on scribbled sky.

Soon sweet will / fill the branches.
Thorns will / graze the arms.

The mother gone, / her voice.
The child-eye's eye will / seize on sound,

resounds her saying / no use to cry.

Before the Newborn Knew Its Wild

A doe white-flags her flight
across the county road and gone.

Her dappled faun wobbles after
as best it can to collapse before my car

and, lying mid-road, curls in head-down
self-erasure (a move I understand)—

the same for car, coyote, or bush-hog blades,
in asphalt road, or tall grass pasture—

makes no struggle being lifted,
no thrash being carried,

unmoving set down on the path
from which it wobbled,

its white-spotted body disappearing
in the leafy half-light.

Kitchen Window

A Carolina wren nested out the window
at the house where children grew,

summer after summer—how long do wrens live?—
I would watch her come and go,
the yellow gape of nestlings' mouths.

Precarious between her claws, she peered in
and we told each other what we knew.

The spring I watch until she does not come,
I find I'd finished my private need
to guard the buried bones:
Queenie's broken pony bones, gerbil bones,
finch bones tinier than sparrow,
and in deep-dug holes mounded smooth,
the horses.
(The time Vaughn set his book across his chest,
I keep seeing the dirt falling on that nice old horse.
Said *old* with such a long *O*.)

And up the hill behind the house,
the good dog bones of Lady.

All day now, in this new place, a wren's whole body
quivers her front-porch song. Beak wide,
she stretches tall, pushes air across her syrinx,
flits chair to redbud, back to wicker—

reminds me—what doesn't?—of me,
the energy I had, my endless repetitions,

and my kitchen-window wren come again
when the kids were young and I helped
her hatchlings fledge.
                      Decades it has been,
and still I set wishbones on the sill above the sink
like tiny flying things lined up to leave.

"Ignorance Is Vastly Underrated."

Vastly.

A red fox or small red coyote
trots along the yard fence,

either way, a predator in daylit bravado.

He pauses to glance around—
the *he* here means *he/she*—*he* being
the default pronoun I had been taught,

accepted without thought
back in boys-will-be-boys days

of *et ux,* and ex-wife with no credit
unless a man co-signed . . .

Ignorance is vastly underrated—
like how pigs slaughtered in France
or veal calves raised right here . . .

Yesterday at the taqueria,
to fork a beef strip off its salad bed,

I flashed to my Hereford cow-calf years,
lifted my fork but did not
not eat the meat,

steering clear of second thought—
how sweet some cows could be,
such good mothers,

(one waited three days at the gate
where her calf disappeared)
how the bottle calves came running,
licking their lips to see me,

the knack I had with the sickly ones,
how many did I save—

and saved for what?

I focused on the bite-sized brown
over-cooked strip,

which is another way to say well done,
ignorance being underrated vastly.

Deep into Present-Day Invisible

After the Barred Owl's nightly questions

but before the promissory notes of wren song
for another dollar day

when window glass slowly surrenders
its reflective—always my best time—

before low-lying white mist dissipates
in warming, as dreams do,
as mine have,

I will stop my walk to look up, deep breathe—
something not done before
what with step counts, A-bombs, late for work,
my period.

Now living beyond my Biblical allotment,
years of surprising sweetness on the tongue's tip,
bitter across the back,

grateful for Irish peasant genes,
and the pale summer solstice moon, its rabbit
the same pale blue of sky,
another wonder.

The Peacock's Tail

For all my binoculared attention
the two white rocks do not
turn to heron.
               What I call a *pond*
remains an algae-pocked stagnation.

Like nothing to be named, a peacock
screams a sound
the first-on-earth might make.
Or last to die.
               And struts his blue exotic
back and forth across the road's soft tar
trailing a tattered tail of seduction
three times his body size.

I have never seen a peahen,
just the cock along the county road
calling out to cars.

Journaling Summer

The dog does not   listen
The cat   carries on

The horses have   gone
Horseless   I carry on

The beautiful   lie
inside   belief
to live in   and die by

as imaginary   god-friend
ends in   an -end

Smell of ripe   peach
nose   to fuzz skin
flesh brightens   in

Praise   song   begun
sweetens   the tongue

Mouth holds   a name
peach douses   all flame

Juice   streaks the chin

The blackberry
bush   of childhood

grown   too tall,
grown not at all

ever mindful   of the time
river water   wrecked

the playground wall

And right on   time
the Norfolk   Southern

sounding down   two miles away
at Browntown

Bougainvillea shedding
blooms   and leaves

A whiff of   someone's burn

A long-legged gray coyote
crossed the walk   -path up ahead

Blood-black scat   with orange seeds
where wild persimmons   fell

Rare here   a bald eagle
high-flying   north, then its mate

My bird app hears   goldfinch
bobolink

I hear   autumn
crickets, smell   promised rain.

Over the New River

Hesitating
at the boulder's edge—
the river so green and flat
and far away—
I had just about decided

when Vaughn hurtled past,
grabbed my hand
and pulled me out and airy
down into the stinging
chill of river.

Our treading water,
looking at each other,
laughing,

and for a long time after,
not quite letting go
I would call upon
the instant of his tug,
my rockless spill,

and I would jump.

The Ruby-Throats Remember Their Flowers, How Long Each Takes to Refill

If we could learn to love
in hummingbird

each to the other's blossoms
deep and sweet

extracting one
from the other's need

alternating bird to blossom,
blossom, bird—here, now here

into each sweet crease
of beloved cover

where murmured words
turn bird—

beige burnished sounds
best expressed in sparrow,

meadowlark, and wren, leaving
awe's brisk and skyward

message to the blue-black
caw of crows.

As Desire Looks to the Future, Regret Implies a Past

What pre-dates desire?
Actually, Vaughn said, *it feels like a relief.*

I used to say the man I loved who died,
now say his name. *Vaughn.*

Two hundred Gaza relief workers
killed in six months. That's a worker a day,

one per diem . . .

    **

Owl faces in walnut pods halved by squirrels.

An artist might collage the oval-eyed,
titled "Gaza," or "Hungry Children."

They say Homer relieved the Iliad's battle
gore with observations of nature.

Rising from the field, the hawk flashes red,
dog-driven from its meal.

The well-fed dogs eat the rabbit.

The fighters call their enemy *Animals*.

The fighting makes them
fighters.

    **

The scientist said, *The answer is the universe.
What we don't know are the questions.*

I understand I will never know,
though embrace the calm of looking up,

and the names I give the shapes
become what I see.

They say *War,*
though from here

it seems more a *Slaughter.*

    **

The solitary raven croaks,
and I croak back.

That the raven croaks again,
that we go back and forth does not
mean a conversation.

And this raven is a raven.
Not anyone I knew who died

as Vaughn came back two times as fox.
Or the same fox twice.

My dogs eat rabbits without hunger,
hard-wired to predate.

Thirteen Couplets in Search of a Water Torture, Love-Your-Neighbor Title

This is not a nature poem
though its speaker walks a farm,

unlookable light greening pastures
for the coming of the cattle.

This is not a farm poem
though cows and fields mentioned

and a small swarm of honeybees lies
beside the path—yes, on the ground—

its lump of queen—injured?—midways
in the docile brown undulating surround,

then a coyote's blood-black scat
laced white with deer hair.

This is not an eat-or-eaten poem.
Not a hunting poem

though everything hunts something.
This is a drip-drip-on-the-forehead

water-torture poem
as the speaker nears the moment

on her farm lane when the neighboring
dog-bark racket marks her passage

and continues its frantic noise
with the speaker well out-of-sight.

Or maybe not. And either way, comes
the speaker's daily *shut-the-f***-up*

thoughts—which must be how
a water-torture poem works. Or not.

Watering Pots in Drought

Another neighbor's dog goes *Woof.*
Desultory.   Listless.
Much white space between *Woof* and *Woof*
as if talking to himself   *Woof.*

A bored *Woof.*   A tired *Woof.*
A making-sure-he's-there *Woof.*
His vinyl needle stuck *Woof.*
One *Woof.*   A commanded by his person *Woof*
or a forgotten-he-had-woofed *Woof*

as I move pot to pot to pot watering
before the coyote dark descends
following the hummingbird
that looks like a bee   *Woof*
(that someone said no, was a moth)
half-burying itself
in purple petunia blooms *Woof.*

Purple to purple, pot to pot on evenings,
even the rainy, I water my pots *Woof*
often tracking a petunia-loving bee/moth.

THREE

Girls' School Reunion: The 50th

We replicate
        our graduation photo
                on the steps of Main,
taller ones behind,
        moving as directed,
                docile as we ever were.
Six of sixty-two have died.
        Evidence remains
                of the boarder/day divide.
She, who said she started
        African Women's Studies
                at her college, who later
danced as if on hot coals
        flailing fists to "Only the Lonely,"
                said, *vulgar*
of my stated need to live
        where I could pee outside.
                No, on second thought,
not *vulgar,*
        her word was *coarse.*
                No need to be so coarse.

Two B-52s Overhead

Training flights to Martinsburg as if the past,
low and loud, never left

The same gray bird perched on the chimney
twilight after twilight
singing of its day

as if the feeder had been seeded

  **

The neighbor's tractor working after dark
headlights back and forth
back and forth

The triangle the Moon, Jupiter, and Saturn will
make this one night
if clouds clear,

the dark here dark enough to see

  **

As cops close in, black kids
marching at the front call out,
White shield! White shield! White shield!

and the white kids surge to take their place
knowing whether cops dark or light
not as rough on white

the color not a color, more than color

    **

A small gray bird singing for itself,
making itself known

Motivation and Learning: Psych 205

I

Second semester in Blodgett's basement,

caged pigeons, row on row, in dim half-light—
the psych syllabus to journal baseline
behavior on free-choice grain.

Food then removed one weekend—we did as told—
and Monday my pigeon soon learned
to peck the paddle, get some grain.
                                     A smart one,
I came to call Petunia. Hunger-driven, I began
messing with her mind.

No other way to say it.
Two pecks. Three. Every other brought reward.
I kept count: kernels, key-pecks.

Described head-bobs. Twirls. Trips around her cage.
All reinforced by kernels dropped.
Or not.

Random reinforcement made her
a wreck of herself in the name of learning. Hers
and mine. I made behavior.

Discovered in me the person who would do this
to a creature I had named
for a flower.

II

Semester over, the TA had said the pigeons
would be gassed—

her orange eyes never blinked
though her pupils widened at my grasping,

this caged creature I had semi-starved
sixteen weeks. Dab of white above her beak.

Iridescent neck. Her soft murmurings.
She stood right where I set her—

first feel of grass?—beneath a campus oak.
Next day, gray breast feathers,

not necessarily pigeon, in the almost perfect
circle of an overhead strike

Dormmate Reunion at Betsy's

At the end of a quiet cul-de-sac,
      a house with laughter and a full life
-time of eclectic art, her own and others.
      Gracie, the rescued whippet.
Plants in pots. Seedlings started.
      The word 'haven' comes to mind.
Of we six, one did not divorce.
      Sally comes in from infusion,
thin but her same deep laugh and smile.
      Susie shows her open-heart scar
puckered raw and red between bare breasts.
      I read them my back room—
now here again—abortion poem.
      Susie asks who the father was.
I shrug. That she can ask, and I can shrug,
      that we can show our scars.

Head-Hunter

First light comes ripe with mysteries
and pungent coyote tracks. I dress for

weather, replenish pockets—dog treats,
cell phone, revolver—in semi-thoughtless rote.

Both dogs scent out in serpentines,
arrive at headless rabbit: full-grown,
therefore savvy (for a rabbit).

Leave it, and they do.

Next day a second headless rabbit,
the first one gone.

Two days later, a starling.

Not a recurring omen, no,
though everything means something.

I go online.

Brains, it seems, the sweet meat
to a long list of nocturnal predators,
owl at the top.

I hear Barred owls here.

Then a male cardinal, his severed head
close to his upturned body
and where his neck ripped off, a hole

perfectly round
as if a fence nail driven in
by a small night stalker, brain devourer

who slurps the best part on the spot
and leaves the rest.

I left the oven on last night.

Out the Kitchen Window, I Find My Dark Side

A mourning dove paces beside the low wall
Baptist preacher-like practicing for Sunday.

Crouched on the wall's other side, the cat sits
fixed as past time.

The dove moves closer to the wall,
stretches its neck, turns, and waddles off.

I relax back to dicing, picturing Coleridge
walking out sound and rhythm

on his Lake District lane. The dove circles back,
again opposite the cat, and this time flutters up.

The cat flashes—both mid-air—and erupting
from my mouth when I would have sworn

all concern for the dove, comes a fist-pumped
YES!

Fallen Fruit

Osage oranges fall *thump* in bright green circles
deer at dusk will come to forage.

Beside the house, a barrage of walnut pods
on gravel: *ping ping ping.*

Jeanette said she quickly learned *rat-tat*
rebel guns from *eh-eh* government ones.

Holed up in her home, huddled against
her bedroom wall, she knew which side

shot into the air, signaling.
                              Later, hiding
up-country near the final rebel checkpoint

rat-tat there meant someone
taken into the trees and killed.

During her year of Red Cross rice,
groveling for G-2 passes,

her pallet on the hut's dirt floor,
she said that *rat-tat* she never got used to.

Nor could she eat the little river fish,
no matter how delicious, for the thought

of the flesh they themselves had eaten.
ping   thump thump.

One Row Ahead: *Fletcher, If You Don't Stop That with Your Sister, You Won't Go to Disney World*

Having started our descent
a shark-like shadow on the broken surface
of an ocean smooth inside itself
skimming past shadows of clouds
the clouds themselves, and a tiny white boat
just the one
              it makes no sense—buckled in
this window seat inside this huge machine
granddaughter beside me inside her earbuds
a steward collecting last-pass trash—
but for a sliver of a moment looking down
I am content for once with being
infinitesimal as a sigh,
transitory as this flight, at one
within the whole of ocean, clouds, and shadows.
Even the pinprick of small white boat
down there so alone.

Morning in Montego Bay

The pile of burning
palm fronds smells like ganja.

        The sun here brought a floater,
just one, to my left eye.

    A man leans, arm extended,
silhouetted against an almond tree, looking out.

Another, swinging a machete,
strolls loose-limbed down the beach.

Arm in arm, a couple slow-walks into the sea,
pauses waist-deep—dark outlines in early light,
turning and returning their bodies to each other.

I feel their savor,
watch the watcher at the sea wall
leaning on the tree.

Two workmen begin raking beach debris
into a wheelbarrow—
                all manner of loss
mixed in flotsam: flipflops, fishnet,
lobster traps, buoys.
            Years ago, his dying.

Black spot in my left eye, I was wrong to think
I had to have it.

      Waft of beach rot mixed with spice
of palm fronds burning.

Far out in a sea lane, a ladened tanker leaving.

A Famous Poet Reads at a D.C. Bookstore

      Not
Robert Frost
at the JFK inaugural—not
as bad as that.

      No sunlit
snow, lost glasses. No hat
held to shade the text.
                      But

bad enough, the poet
stumbling lost
in his word-forest,
            lost

in pauses long as sorrow, his lost
corduroy pants
holding crumpled proof of what
had been as I worked to extract

his meant
threads, my gut pitted tight.
        Then in the straining quiet

he clearly said, *White*
is whiter in the dark,
and there stood my dream-white
horse on a no-moon night.

Atrophied, said the Gynecologist

All gone: the geese, the ducks, the great grays.
It's gotten quiet here. Dry and quiet.

The inner once-upon-a-time grew tired.
Tiredness kept growing,

lugging all that expectation every which way
in late summer of the mind.
                                 Night sirens
cannot find whoever pulls the covers up,
turns to story:
                 the shadow-seeming crow
perched on a fence. The bush that seems coyote.

The cow that is, black and placid-walking
a second following, calf in line behind,
all nodding yes, yes, yes.

Birds flit in, check the summer feeder—
what has been might come again.

The black not-a-stick bites the dog,
disappears in a patch of lamb's ear.

In the gratitude desk the gift of solitude
lies in the keyhole drawer.

A dreamed road, a high-banked ancient path.
Cattle on both sides. White here.

Black there. Wire fence, less impediment
than idea.
   Mid-road, a small white calf
I shoo in with the black.
A white cow lies moaning on the verge.
I nudge her up,
     find a black calf underneath,
almost herd them to the whites

when a Barred owl wakes me.

Some days I think: *Come back, come back.*
Others, not so much,
     having lived certain
plot points of long marriage.

The dogwood, its bark stripped,
limbs sprouting below the antler damage,
dead above.
    Why not a dogwood bush
if it wants that much to live?

Look into the future's open mouth
its uvula waggles like a lure,
a tasty lure that beckons, *Come and get it.*

All Day on the Farm

     All day the dark
rests up. Diminished, yes,
but waiting
in the growing season,
the summer of the mind.
     Meanwhile,
unwrap another given,
careful of its fragile.
     Can you hear
the meter running,
numbers
counting down?

     **

     New growth
sprouting
as ideas will build this
from that,
leaf from twig, no *this*
without first *that*.

     **

     If I had a pipe
to put it in, I'd suck the savor:
taste buds flowering,
peepers starting up,
still ponds still

only on the surface,
daffodils, one tiny honeybee.

**

    I notice what I know.
The rest: background chirps
and warbles.
    The slap of flipflops
follows me around.

**

    It continues as before.
All of it.
On and on without.
    Rock outcrops persist
their dulling of bushhog blades.
    Thistles whack-a-mole
across the fields as always,
    and days break open
orange-turned-white
    of fried eggs.
    Geese wings *whoosh
whoosh* away.

**

    It all continues
as before.

    And not.

    Pasture grasses grow
without becoming
        round-bales.
Cattle
    but a neighbor's.

      **

    It could be bare
bone lonely here

if not

one's best self
in solitude.

    And this.
If not
    for this. For this
from that.

After Anguish

      Barn stalls gape empty,
draped with cobwebs.
      The time for burrowing
soft and deep, quilt to chin, under scraps
patched to pattern: cathedral window's
twelve-fold squares.
      In early dark and deepening
chill, trees blacken against the gray,
a western tint of light remaining.
      Here it's time to settle
into quiet, flame reducing to ember,
just as hot.

      My own careful fire, small
and flickering, cup hands around—
never mind the old black book
of should-ought-don't in large
bold print.
      I will read in expectation.
Let joy winnow from despair
as grain separates from husk. Satisfy my
craving thick soups, mashed potatoes,
ice cream straight from the carton.
      Spend early evenings cradling
stemmed bowls of pinot noir
gleaming in firelight.

      With the next warm day—

maybe tomorrow—I intend to go out,
gaze into the calming sky—

it always helps—
look up with trust the way I rode my last
good horse those years ago.

    I will wait out the deepening
winter for hummingbirds' return,
for zinnia, cleome to reseed themselves.

    Twice a day, walk the dogs
around these farm fields, noticing
what's here and now, outside myself,
and with any luck and time—
if I am given time—give it all
another go.

Notes

The Taylor place in "Wheat Straw for Bedding Horse Stalls" is Henry Taylor's home place near Lincoln, VA where his father Tom farmed. Henry won the Pulitzer for his collection *The Flying Change*.

"A Famous Poet Reads at a D.C. Bookstore" refers to Robert Frost's difficulty reading the poem he wrote for John F. Kennedy's inauguration. The strong reflected sunlight after the snowstorm made his words impossible to decipher as he stood on the podium. He ended up reciting something else.

"Motivation and Learning: Psych 205" is for Diane Vaughan, my lab partner whom I wrote out of this piece for her sake as well as the poem's.

"Dormmate Reunion at Betsy's" is for Betsy Goodman Belz, Suzanne Dyer Wise, Neelie Caminati Gray, Diane Wise Vaughan (again), and the late Sally Goodman Graflund.

"Fallen Fruit" is for my Liberian colleague, Jeanette Ebba Davidson, who went missing during the Civil War but with luck and brains survived to tell me her story.

"Fruitful" was inspired by Ross Gay's wonderful "To the Fig Tree at 9th and Christian" that got me thinking about fruit poems.

"Ignorance is Vastly Underrated" comes from an opinion piece by Peter Coy "Sure, Knowledge Is Power, but Ignorance Is Underrated." in the New York Times, June 21, 2024.

About the Author

Wendell Hawken came to poetry late in life earning her MFA from Warren Wilson College's Program for Writers decades after her Vassar College BA. Her time in the Warren Wilson MFA program, founded by Ellen Bryant Voigt, changed her life with its brilliance and rigor, and gave her a lifelong place in the Wally tribe.

To date, her publications include two chapbooks and five full collections. *From a Spit Seed* is her sixth.

In 2023, Hawken was named the inaugural Poet Laureate of Millwood VA, an unincorporated quirky village in the northern Shenandoah Valley where she lives on a grass farm with two Labradoodles and a rescued beagle named Beagle. She promotes poetry with quarterly open-mic gatherings, posting poems in public spaces, and writing poems to commemorate community events.

www.ingramcontent.com/pod-product-compliance
Lightning Source LLC
Chambersburg PA
CBHW071011160426
43193CB00012B/2003